Blockchain Technology: The Future

30 Minutes Read

Deepak Gupta

Published by Inspirational Publishing, 2022.

Table of Contents

1. Title Page 1

2. Copyright © Deepak Gupta 2022 3

4. Note for the Readers: This Book isn't Financial Advice but Fact-Based Elaboration! 5

5. Prologue 7

6. The Blockchain Technology: Futuristic Opportunity!.... 9

7. Understanding Blockchain Technology 11

8. Cryptocurrency: The Present and Future! 13

9. Stocks or Cryptocurrency: Which One is Most Reliable! 17

10. Blind Follow Sheep Walk in Crypto! 19

11. Money Generation: Who Will Claim the Money First! 21

12. Will Cryptocurrency Ever Reach the Future! Or Does it Really Deserve a Future? 23

13. NFTs: Non-Fungible Tokens 27

14. Can You Really Sell NFTs? How Feasible is the Idea! Why Should Someone Buy a Digital File? 29

15. Metaverse 33

16. Is Metaverse Really Possible in the 21st Century? 37

17. Decentralised Finance: Defi 39

18. Can You Keep Your Money as Defi! 41

19. Web 3.0: The Third Generation of the Internet 43

20. FINAL VERDICT ON BLOCKCHAIN TECHNOLOGY 47

21. About the Author 49

BLOCKCHAIN

TECHNOLOGY

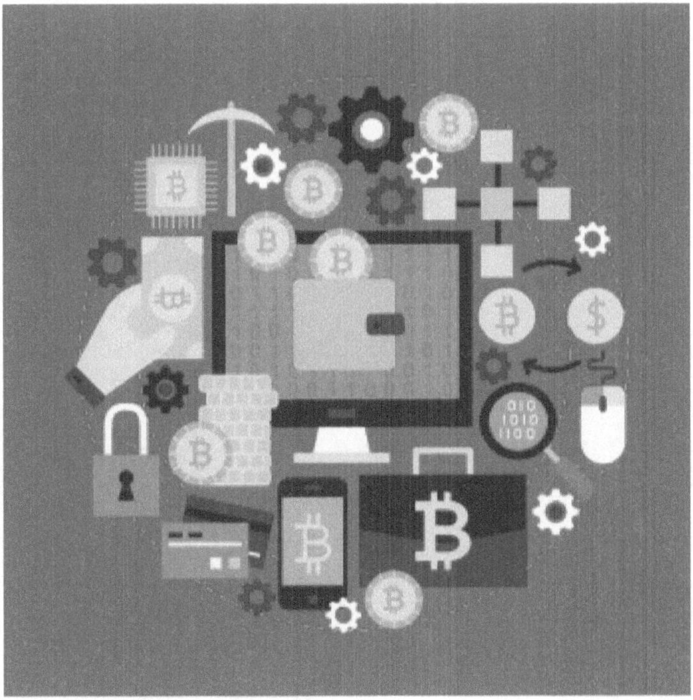

THE FUTURE
DEEPAK GUPTA

Copyright © Deepak Gupta 2022

Note for the Readers: This Book isn't Financial Advice but Fact-Based Elaboration!

1. Kindly understand, this book isn't financial advice but entirely based on facts. We have conducted extensive research to make this book practical to read and perceive. In addition, we will not be responsible for any loss or damage anyone would incur while following or interpreting this book.

2. In addition, this is not a promotional book. The names we have used in the book are used to clarify the happening of events and methods.

3. The book is possibly error free. The Publishers and Authors will not be responsible for any loss or damage to anyone caused by the content of the book.

Prologue

Getting rich overnight was a dream till the concept of blockchain introduced in our cultured world, but it's sheer injustice to Blockchain Technology if we only appreciate the concept of Cryptocurrency only. Blockchain Technology has given birth to many novel revolutionary concepts where the dream of becoming rich has become a big reality. When everyone had the fantasy of becoming rich overnight, the volatility factory of Cryptocurrency made it possible to earn an staggering amount of money in a matter of few minutes. When stock traders were earning a slight amount of return after analysing and sweating to discuss every company's opportunities and future, bitcoin commenced its journey in 2009. Some people bought Bitcoins and became millionaires in a few years. When magic becomes real, the game transforms. Now, the bubble of crypto has been rising like fire in the woods, but is it really legitimate according to every country's Government, where only a few will get money and more will lose. The question of legalization and accepting Blockchain is churning the minds of everyone where there's a lot of hustle and bustle because to get returns, most people are investing their hard-earned money in hopes of getting good returns and forgetting the risk attached with it. When someone said to us, we have made ten lakhs from ten thousand in a year, then we would laugh at him because it's looking quite impossible and resembling a fraud scheme, so most people would deny the scheme but as the blockchain technology introduced Cryptocurrency, the reality to earn enormous amount of money is making people half-blind to lose everything to becoming rich some night. And that's why most people are ready to lose, because that's the risk. *The possibility of impossibility is attracting many investors all over the world where the bubble is getting huge every day.*

Likewise, blockchain technology has also given birth to ***Metaverse, NFTs, Decentralized Finance and web 3.0***, and people are noting them as a future technology but how much we can rely on them, that's a brilliant question. Our world is recognized for its practicality, but this technology is entirely on a virtual basis, so it's interesting to know how we would accept it in our real world. A lot of opportunities and challenges are still emerging on the micro and macro level. ***When there's an opportunity to earn a huge return, sometimes the blind rule follows where even a fool tries to earn something out of it.*** Consequently, it's strenuous to know whether it's an intelligent race or a sheep race. If we look closely, most people don't even know about this technology and investing money without a clue. Like if we eliminate money from blockchain technology, most people will run away with their money. **We aren't thinking negatively, but practically. This book is totally based on a practical and feasible approach to understanding whether it's undoubtedly water or a mirage in the desert.**

The Blockchain Technology: Futuristic Opportunity!

If someone asks us about the fundamental definition of Blockchain, then our tongues may get confused to depict it in a simple manner. Even most people don't know about blockchain but are still investing in Cryptocurrency by following the blind rule. Blockchain Technology is really an old concept and it was introduced by **two researchers, Stuart Haber and W. Scott. Stornetta in 1991** and until then we were living in web 1.0 where we could read only. Web 1.0 is the flat system where people can see and read. There was nothing like interaction like we do in today's time on the web. As the technology wasn't effectively developed, we had the concept but not the feasibility of it. Like today, we have cars and we are working on flying cars. *The first implementation of Blockchain Technology was done in Jan 2009 when Bitcoin launched as a first real-world implementation. And someone mentioned it right, there's always a first mover advantage on the internet.* No one had ever thought that a few bitcoins for just a few bucks could make anyone a millionaire in very little time. And like wise, with popularity and time, people started investing and new crypto coins got launched in a very short span. In crypto market, you can experience many coins like **Bitcoin, Ethereum, Gala, Mana Decentraland, Loopring, Dogecoin, Shiba Inu, Sandbox, and many more.** Every coin has some purpose like recently Elon Musk introduced some merchandise that could buy with doge coins. Presently anyone can buy virtual land in the metaverse with Sandbox and Gala coins. As when people buy coins, the cryptocurrency market goes up and people's return on investment rises. Overall, the well-connected world is accepting Blockchain Technology slowly, but also the views on it aren't quite similar. Recently, China banned cryptocurrency activities including mining, but some countries like *El Salvador became the first brave country to accept Bitcoin as legal tender on June 9, 2021*. Nayib Bukele, the president of El Salvador, sees a future in crypto and has legalized using it instead of money, but some countries are still combating it over the decision to treat it as an asset class. Now, confusion has started in India over *whether crypto is legal or not*. Not in India, but also all over the world; people are treating it as lottery and gambling activities.

Understanding Blockchain Technology

B lockchain Technology is the decentralised system where information gets electronically stored in various blocks. It's a distributed, secured and safe database in which every new transaction gets recorded in blocks in seconds (even in microseconds). *In simple terms, it's a chain of information, and every time a new information is added, a new block is also generated and there's no ending to that.* Blocks are the storage capacities where new information gets added from periodically. Blockchain Technology is majorly used in Cryptocurrency where people can buy various coins and can get returns over time. We will get to the crypto discussion later. Blockchain was first used for Bitcoin in 2009 and we all know the result of it. In the above definition, I mentioned decentralised system; it means there's no centre that is controlling Blockchain. *It's an entire decentralised system of users with no intermediary in between.* Investors and buyers have full control of decisions and liquidation of their funds. It's an absolute transparent system of the valid information. When someone buys crypto, information of its every kind gets stored in blocks forever and the keys are so strong that it's practically impossible to alter. Nothing will get erased and can't be changed possibly. Moreover, some people say blockchain transactions can be altered, but it's extremely challenging to do.

Majority of people are seeing blockchain as negative for the economy because the concept of Cryptocurrency has washed the mind of some people, so to have clarity of thought, we need a stable mind that can think above money and sheep race. *You know, there are 20 million crypto investors in India and it's astonishing to know that India has the most number of crypto investors in the world. Moreover, there are 50 million crypto investors around the globe.* As a result, the issue of crypto has now gone to a serious level where banning it directly can't solve the issue.

Cryptocurrency: The Present and Future!

Everyone wants to be rich and if possible, as soon as possible, that's the symbolic sign of Cryptocurrency which is inducing huge investors from all over the world, especially from India. Most industries see India as a massive market because 140 crore people really depict an unbelievable number, *even if someone sells a single rupee product to all citizens, the entrepreneurs will get 140 crores in one go.* In India, the competition is stiff, and it's hard to make money easily. And here we are talking about crypto, where people are investing a huge amount of money in the expectation of being rich in a short span of time. Of course, crypto made it possible. No denial. A few years back, the government of most countries were never interested in knowing the Cryptocurrency because the investors were too less to make impact on the economy on micro and macro level but as the thirst to get money increased, Government really wants to regulate it to maintain stability in the country. Like a stock market that keeps the power to uplift and destroy any economy, crypto-extreme volatility can make anyone rich or beggar overnight. *No joke, that's the truth. There are both sides of coin.* Recently China and some other countries banned crypto, while the country of El Salvador became the first to identify it as legal tender like we mentioned before.

Let's see how regulations work! The classification of crypto falls into two categories: *one is like a legal tender and the second as an asset class.* Legal tender means the currency can be used instead of rupees to make payments. No one can deny legal tender of the country while being as an asset class; the crypto will be used as an investment, i.e. people can buy, sell, hold or even use to make payments like buying NFTs. It can be used as a means of exchange to access goods and services. Crypto doesn't rely on banks to verify transactions as there's no mediator in between. It's a peer to peer system. Therefore, if someone buys crypto, his information will be stored permanently.

Now, when 20 million people came into action, the Indian government came into action. *In 2018, RBI banned Cryptocurrency but supreme court of India rescinded the ban by saying, we can't ban it just because we don't grasp it right now.* The ban isn't the solution. As India has enormous number of investors, the multiple misleading fearful information mostly lead to the market decline where the big sharks had withdrawn their money and market got crashed multiple times. And in between, most investors got covered in almost half their losses. *Till the market was running up, everyone was extremely delighted, but as the market went down, people got panicked, but that's the nature of the cryptocurrency market, the volatility. It can go up as quickly as it can and go down and may even go to zero.* The crypto market needs huge money every day to make investors happy, but in the misleading information age, the cryptocurrency market goes down every day. So, we can assume, most investors work only on the legs of other investors where if no one invests then no one will, while if you are dealing in stock market, you need considerable thinking skills to analyse and understand the past, present and future of companies. Investors have to find out potential and future possibilities. Affirmative, the crypto market also has predictions like if someone buys the virtual asset in Decentraland Mana, the mana coin will go up but most coins fail to make significant impact on the market. **Every coin has a purpose, but purpose alone can't meet the needs of investors.**

In blockchain technology, you will not find any mediator, and that's it's power and weakness too. As there's only buyers and sellers in the Cryptocurrency market, they can manipulate the market by luring other people to invest while making a group to show fake returns or can trigger some kind of trading because mostly daily investors always look for fast trading and in that between, the innocent people face loses. *It's valid that multiple groups of buyers can manipulate the market in their own way.*

With a lot of ups and downs, currently Russia is calling for banning crypto and in India, with the Budget proposal of 2022, **crypto is being taxed at flat 30% on profit and losses can't be set off to any year plus 1% TDS on every transaction.** If we look deeply, we will find the government will not be letting away investors who have already been holding their money and making a big return on that. The tax is chiefly for early investors who have been making returns while holding since 2018 or before. It's undoubtedly an extremely clever and aggressive approach by the government. Right now, the people who have invested in crypto are shivering but still our Finance Minister Nirmala Sitharaman has cleared that taxing crypto isn't a step towards banning or regulation of Cryptocurrency. Also, our deputy RBI governor is repeatedly calling to ban crypto by observing it as a Ponzi scheme and the best decision that can be done is to ban crypto to prevent funnelling money and instability of economy. In recent Indian Budget 2022, it was mentioned, RBI will issue digital rupee legal tender based on blockchain technology in 2022-23 and will be supported by **Central Bank Digital Currency (CBDC)**. The currency will be different than that of paper currency.

Stocks or Cryptocurrency: Which One is Most Reliable!

A few months back, our former RBI Governor Raghuram Rajan said, crypto is a bubble that will burst soon and remember, until there's one similar view on blockchain technology, it would not survive. ***This is not financial advice but factual advice.*** Stocks are exclusively based on company's performance. There are extreme discussions behind buying and selling of stocks. Shares or any kind of financial instruments have some basis to take decisions. They have logic, basis, understanding, thinking and clarity, while in crypto, there's no base to make it stable. Most people are purely for money. ***Crypto is a 24-hour market where most investors don't sleep peacefully after investing their hard-earned money, but also there's huge returns too.*** Why would someone go for stocks when they have huge returns in Cryptocurrency market and that's the question! The world is changing and adapting swiftly. People are ready to take big risks in a short span of time while ignoring good returns in a long period of time. This sense depicts the harsh greediness of making fast money and becoming rich overnight. And that's why the cryptocurrency bubble is increasing. Everyone has hope, and everyone is trying their luck with money. Investing 10,000 bucks can give you 10 lakh bucks and, in that hope, and luck, people are even ready to lose their 10,000 bucks happily. Welcome to the 21st century, where most people don't invest in stocks because it requires intelligence and mostly only a few wants to devote too much time. ***Even people are shifting from stocks to crypto because it's beating the returns.*** For medium risk, the share market is good with extremely good returns with medium risk in a very long-time span, but crypto can make the returns quick to peak or to zero in no time.

Blind Follow Sheep
Walk in Crypto!

It's not the first time when people are getting huge returns on their investments; even when the Cryptocurrency wasn't here, people were earning extremely huge money with other ways. Stocks are the oldest concept of share market even when the internet wasn't introduced still most of the people aren't interested to enter the share market because it requires a deep level of analysis, thinking, intelligence and predictions, so it's not everyone's cup of tea and even after if you pass in all, you will not get that huge returns easily in a short span of time. If you are a Cryptocurrency investor, you will understand that there's no stability in Cryptocurrency market, either the market goes up or it goes down. *There's nothing like stable prices, and it happens because most investors follow each other than using their own minds.* Mostly, the cryptocurrency market doesn't need too much understanding like the share market. You too alone can't make a big thought in it. Multiple people should have the same thinking to get the market goes up. So, when everyone puts money into the market, the market goes up, and when everyone withdraws, the market goes down. The masses follow the rules, so, individual thoughts don't matter in Crypto in the short run. Most people are only for fast money and follow the market scenario; only, even multiple groups of people can manipulate *Cryptocurrency market to lure small investors to put their money into the market, and who doesn't like huge returns? That's why the market is still alive.* The Blockchain Technology is marvellous and can help to build the future, but the base of this technology should get run in the long span.

Money Generation: Who Will Claim the Money First!

When Cryptocurrency makes 90% of people poor, then 10% of people become rich.

When a business raises funds from the market, it utilises money in projects, earns profit, and gives reasonable returns to investors. There's value generation in business projects. So, business doesn't need money every time to grow; it needs good projects, and finally it benefits the investors but if we look closely, in Crypto market, there's no such value generation where money isn't bringing profits but money is only attracting money. It's like everyone is just placing bricks to build a long wall and there's no value generation. When most people lose, only a few become rich because when the Cryptocurrency Sea was created, there were no sharks but now these sharks are eating new fishes to get extremely huge returns and that's why everyone is at loss. Think if someone gets 100 times the returns on their investments, then what will happen to the new investors because in Solana, Gala and Dogecoin people did the same rule and the early birds flew away with all the money.

Now, understand, we aren't against the Cryptocurrency market, but analysing it at an unbiased level. I'm also a substantial investor in the cryptocurrency market. *In Crypto market, there's a concept to HODL, yes, it's hodl not hold. HODL means hold it for dear life.* In other words, it says to hold the coins even in adverse situations to get profitable returns in a long time. But the question is, who will claim the money first! Suppose there are ten people who want to invest 100 each in a coin in Crypto. And every time they invest, the market will go up, obviously. Now almost nine people will be profiting at different returns and the highest returns will go to early investors. Don't forget that all investors have some profit, but they all are holding in hope of getting more returns. So, it means all are claiming the same money, but it's still on the market. When negativity spreads in the market, the old investors who have become sharks, withdraw their money with huge returns; almost 6-7 will be at loss because now the money has moved out from the market. *Our former RBI Governor Raghuram Rajan said, it's the bubble that will burst soon and that's the vital problem in Cryptocurrency market. Everyone feels they are in profit, but actually it's the same money that makes feel everyone satisfied. It's the common money, and those who will claim first, will get returns, and others have to wait for other people's investment, and when the market goes up, they will get the chance to withdraw.* There's nothing like any value that bringing money in the market except some NFTs and Metaverse projects.

In Cryptocurrency market, everyone is claiming the same money where out of 100% people, only 10% will become rich and I think 10% is still more.

Will Cryptocurrency Ever Reach the Future! Or Does it Really Deserve a Future?

The crypto market doesn't work on value creation but on money stuffing. So, it needs a huge number of people around the globe to make survival, and everyone should feel good about it because only the huge investors can make the market up to have a profitable situation for everyone. And even this market was growing in the past because everyone had some belief in getting huge returns. We need similar views on Cryptocurrency whether we regulate, legalize, or ban it. As we said, the government has taxed Cryptocurrency in India at 30% tax with no set-off losses for any year and also 1% TDS on every Crypto transaction. It's the strategy of Indian government to not let go people whose portfolios are in huge returns and they are still holding it proudly. It's a clear indication to force sell and ordering them to exit the market, so when they exit, the market will get crashed and it would be easy for them to ban it. *Recently China banned Cryptocurrency and Russia called for ban but we can't also ignore the countries like Denmark, UK, Spain,*

Mexico, Japan, Iceland, Germany and France whose Cryptocurrency systems are regulated well. Every country is dealing with Crypto at their own level. We all know, Cryptocurrency is a decentralized platform where the government has no control over it, so it's fascinating to know how the government will manage a decentralized platform and make it centralized and regulated.

Acknowledge a Few Points Before Reading Ahead:

1. There's a lot of dissimilarities in Cryptocurrency view. We need a single approach to deal with it, but it's terribly problematic to implement the similar rules across the globe and expect the best regulations.

2. Everyone thinks in Cryptocurrency market that they can become rich very soon. People are seeing it as a way to make fast money and ignoring the extremely high risk of losing every single penny in a second. While investing in Cryptocurrency, everyone should understand Cryptocurrency isn't the way to make fast money.

3. The strong point of Crypto is the volatility factor and everyone worships that. May be one day your portfolio can be on 40% loss and next day on 40% profit but when there's dissimilarities in the market, the new investors suffer because the old investors take out extremely huge money from the market. To get everyone profitable in their portfolios; Crypto market should go on long without making an interruption in between. With conflicts, it can eat up everything, and people will get the fear factor in their minds. Everyone has to wait to become sharks, but it would happen when the sea survives.

4. As we all know, mostly the youth are investing money in the Crypto market. The question is, everyone is running towards money, so where's the process of the sense of achievement where youth learns something to understand the value of everything. What will be the future of youth! Yes, everyone has the right to make money, but Crypto is the way to make money only, and no value is being distributed to the youth.

5. For regulations, the government has to protect youth at the individual level. Most young people are losing sleep over stress and in fear of a declining market. The jumping market depicts jumping heartbeats. At a national level, the government wants to protect family savings because most youngsters are trying eating up family savings while giving a blind hope to become rich one day. At the national level, it can bring threats like terrorism, prostitution, money laundering even after the identified block chain transactions. Also, the stability of the economy is also dependent on the crypto-market. As we already said, sometimes big investors lure small investors to invest money in the market and they lose money in the hope.

6. In the market, the same money shows multiple investors the same gains, but in reality, the gain will go to the ones who will claim it first. (Early Bird Approach)

7. With aggressive tax strategy, the Indian government is discouraging people to invest and also trying to take huge tax from investors who are still holding their money. Remember, our Indian government is gradually creating understanding of Crypto market while building the thoughts in our minds, so if something bad happens, they will take the decision to ban and it will not feel quick to anyone.

8. Like, before adopting anything, we should learn about it; likewise, we should also understand the concept of Crypto; it's benefits, how it works, the risk associated with it and everything because the overnight money can make almost anyone blind.

9. Like the stock market closes at a fixed time, there should be a right time when market gets closed and everyone can get the good opportunity to spend time happily and get a peaceful sleep. The 24-hour money-making scheme has swept away the sleep of most youngsters. Money is significant but not as significant as health.

NFTs: Non-Fungible Tokens

Have you heard about Picasso, whose paintings were sold for millions of dollars and yet people are still mad about them? Put differently, the arts are extremely valuable that give the sense and hope of life to human beings. Most people buy paintings as a collection and display it exclusively in their homes. *Arts have deep meanings and there's no question about; what is the art! Because its art and it can be made with any vision.* Significantly, arts have deep details for which they are sold or get auctioned for huge prices. Some painters even died poor while their arts were sold for billions after that. That's intermittently the problem with the arts; people discover their meanings too late. Most arts have dynamic perceiving power. Some perceive it differently, while some as a similar view. Before NFTs were launched, most paintings had only a unique copy and whoever offered the most reasonable price, would own it. Now, when blockchain technology was introduced, no one had ever thought that a tweet would get sold for lakhs of dollars or bored ape pictures could sell for millions! That's the art of valuation! No one can assume the price of an art. It can be valuable or invaluable.

Recently, a 22-year-old Indonesian college student sold his 5-year selfies for millions, and now, he's confused about what he would describe his parents about the money. It's difficult to explain blockchain technology to people who haven't even heard of it. NFTs are Non-Fungible Tokens, mostly known in its short form. These are assets that use blockchain technology and are stored in a digital ledger. It's like selling digital tokens and earn money after selling it. You can sell or trade photos, art, videos or music. Suppose you have made a digital art and you want to sell it to someone without losing the sense of copyright; then you can mint your art in marketplaces like Opensea or Rarible. When you publish your art using blockchain technology, it gets stored there as tokens and this process is known as minting. Opensea and Rarible are just the platforms to transfer assets. They don't own any of the assets but work with metamasks and other wallets. Sometimes these platforms charge Gas Fees for the smooth working of chains like Ethereum or Polygon. Now, when you sell your art to someone, you will have to pay some gas fees and a small commission to the platform, like 2.5% of the selling price. In blockchain technology, it's always mentioned that it's you when the first time you minted the art. Your name will always be mentioned, and you will get a fixed commission on every time your art gets sold by the next buyer. So, **primarily NFTs are investments that bring royalties to the old owner and as well as the person who last sold that item.** You can also do a giveaway and transfer the NFT to anyone's metamask wallet address.

Can You Really Sell NFTs? How Feasible is the Idea! Why Should Someone Buy a Digital File?

When an NFT is listed, mostly art and photos are visible. They aren't physical paintings where piracy can be avoided even though someone has the digital copy of it. People can take the screenshots from Photos and Arts, make a lavish printout, and hang it on their walls. What's so special! Why would someone give millions just to hang paintings in their homes? *First*, NFT isn't an expenditure but an investment. It means your art should be sellable, and most people should feel it as an investment. In the digital world, everyone is making art and there's a lot of extremely passionate people who are experts in building great designs and art. So, every time you think about selling an NFT, think about the whole competition. *It's easy to mint an art but extremely difficult to sell if someone doesn't feel its value as an investment.* Usually, some NFTs got viral before they got sold because when an art gets popular, people run to buy them as it will make money on selling due to its popularity.

So, make something that can become the talk of the town and then collectors will surely buy your NFTs.

When you explore the NFTs market, you will find, some NFTs are cheap while some are extremely expensive. ***When you find difficult to value something, it will surely be an investment.*** Remember that. The competition is really stiff, so telling and predicting what will happen in the future, is like judging without testing the water.

Also, even if someone screenshots your NFT, ownership will remain with you because it's already stored as tokens in the blockchain. It's irreversible and can't be obliterated easily from the metamask or other wallets. Its Non-Fungible means Non exchangeable Tokens. One thing we noted is that collectors can't modify the NFTs. They can just have the right to sell, trade, or transfer the tokens.

The Noticeable Vital Points about NFTs:

1. There's no intermediary that supports the NFTs marketplace except some platforms, but they just work on their limits. Some buyers and sellers can manipulate prices to show NFT as valuable to persuade collectors.

2. Most of the artists are minting NFTs in the hope of selling at higher prices, but it's extremely tougher than we think. NFTs are an investment, like your NFTs have some value to sell for more in future because no one wants to hang one-million-dollar art on their wall just to show off to some people except some passionate art collectors.

3. If you want to secure your art even without listing it for sale, then NFTs platforms are best to make your art safe and you still own the rights even when someone copies it. You can even have the right to sue in case of misuse. So, blockchain is transparent and secure to keep arts as yours forever.

4. Don't you think people want exclusive rights to have a paper painting than a digital painting? It's tough to accept because having art in digital form and as a detailed painting on walls is too different. Reactions to these situations are thoroughly mixed.

5. NFTs can be sold by creativity and uniqueness and don't forget competition is stiff because you are competing with the world's best artists.

6. Is it possible to set the price of an NFT? Can you judge the correctness of the price? No, because everyone perceives art differently! For someone it can be extremely valuable and for someone, it's nothing. Digital art can be used as an investment and nothing else.

7. Remember, most NFTs get sold when their value feels extremely higher than the price set by the artists.

8. There's always a fixed royalty to the original creator every time the NFT gets sold.

9. Till now, the most expensive NFT ever sold is The Merge, which was sold on Nifty gateway between 2 December & 4 December 2021 for $91.8 Million and that was held by 28,983 collectors. That's the power of art and the digital world. Also, crypto-punk is among the expensive NFTs in the world.

Metaverse

You know, the internet is our lifeline to innovations and developments, but we have never thought that one day we have to live inside the internet to understand our lives. Very well, you heard it right. Unlimited resources exist only on the internet, and the only three-dimensional world exists is our reality, but it's essential to note, everything is an investment in blockchain technology. When the cryptocurrency was launched as bitcoin in 2010, no one believed that it would survive, but as time moved, the concept made everyone mad and many people became billionaires. Who doesn't want to be rich! Everyone wants to. Most people regret to miss this opportunity, now every time a new concept is introduced in blockchain, people get rushed to buy and hold anything as an investment. The trust in blockchain technology is mostly the positivity of the majority of people. Do you ever want to buy a virtual property that has no real connection to the physical world? Possibly No, of course you can interact with virtuality, but only mentally. Is it possible to connect the real world with virtual reality? Many people are purchasing virtual plots and lands for investment so that they can sell them for more. Every blockchain technology just aims at bringing money for people. Now people don't want to lose the opportunity to become rich, and even they are ready to lose money.

Metaverse is a simulated digital environment which is based on the combination of Virtual Reality (VR) and Augmented Reality (AR). It's like a 3D virtual fictional world where people are securing their virtual land and properties represented by NFTs. It's virtuality is a big challenge in the 21st century. Where we are already losing physical touch in the internet world, people are getting surrounded by gadgets and we are moving towards a metaverse where people gather to meet mentally than physically. Even anyone can hang out with celebrities without an issue. Most metaverses are in the form of NFTs, and you can buy a plot at a rate like $10,000. Using this blockchain technology, people are making money like a real world where you can do online shopping, hang out with people, set up online games to play or get played. Basically, it's creating a parallel world where you can do anything almost mentally by sitting on your couch. You can buy land and then rent it to someone and he can open a shop for any business. An e-commerce business can also be opened. Even virtual art galleries are getting preferences before purchasing. Just like real banners, you can advertise your business on virtual banners. So, mentally, information can be transferred in any form.

Even web 3.0 is the foundation of the metaverse. Now, Facebook, Instagram and WhatsApp are resembling their businesses as Meta. You know, Internet is a two-dimensional world while our real world is three-dimensional. It means our physical world is more interactive than the internet but as metaverse introduced, the three-dimensional virtual world is giving tough competition, but it's possible, when more people believe this technology, then it can go forward. On the internet, you see texts, images, and videos, but now physical reality is combining with virtual reality with multiple sensors like a real hologram. I think you know how we experience holograms in real life. Metaverse is practically interactive with the real environment.

You can buy metaverse with Crypto coins like Ethereum, Gala, Mana Decentraland, Enjin Coin or Sandbox. *When people buy metaverse, the cryptocurrency market goes up and that's the investment in metaverse.*

Is Metaverse Really Possible in the 21st Century?

A virtual world is fast but can make real world lazy, so while having metaverse, we need a lot of discipline but also, we can't forget the fact that lands of metaverse are cheaper as compare to a real world but it's hard to hold them as investment when you can't explain why you have such virtual property where we can't touch a single thing.

Remember, it's extremely challenging to live in the virtual and real world simultaneously because when you enter the virtual world, you have to escape reality. The reality is significant. *Most people are in blockchain technology to make a lot of money, and that's why it's growing like hell.*

Decentralised Finance: Defi

When banks were not introduced, people used to hold on to their money in their pockets as savings or made a gullak to save money but idle money doesn't generate anything, and even inflation eats up its value overtime. As a result, it's really significant to stop time of your finances. Also, in olden times, the government didn't have proper records to receive taxes correctly, effectively and regularly. So, financial institutions were introduced to keep the financial data to access micro and macro-financial positions. Banks and other financial institutions are centralized finance where the public have to follow the terms and conditions and the rules related to it. With blockchain technology, many worlds have been changing including the system of centralised finance.

Decentralised Finance popularly known as Defi, can hold your money in a secure digital bank than keeping it in a centralised bank. It eliminates bank fees and the rules of how your money is kept and used in banks. In centralized systems, the guidelines are strict and taxes can't be evaded but Defi is an open & transparent financial system secured with distributed ledgers where people will get higher interest rates and pay low transaction charges. Most significantly, it eliminates middlemen in financial transactions with having a peer-to-peer financial system. Basically, it uses digital currency where there's no bank or broker. Every time you purchase something; you use a digital wallet to make payments.

Can You Keep Your Money as Defi!

Defi *is a brilliant platform, but applying the same rules and regulations all over the globe is a sense of foolishness because every country's public has diverse patterns of keeping their money.* Relying solely on Defi is risky as different decentralised companies have their own rules and regulations! As it's decentralised, the government will always interfere to know what's actually happening with public money. It's some kind of risk to leave money in the hands of decentralized finance, but considering it as a future, we see it as a big opportunity. It can work best with a centralized system where people will get a choice to keep their money where they want it. Also, Defi is a secured platform, but it's difficult to know how much money someone is holding in different digital wallets. So, it may be a hassle for the government to find out who is playing with them. To get executed, the same rules should be implemented, at least a few to have similarities of working as decentralized finance, just like centralized. Overall, we can understand, Defi is like a liberalised form of Cefi.

Web 3.0: The Third Generation of the Internet

The human world is changing faster than the development of the internet. Earlier, people worked at offices and enjoyed themselves at home. Now they work at home and go outside to enjoy themselves. You know, **Web 3.0 is the third generation of the internet and before that we had web 1.0 and web 2.0.** Before 2000, we had web 1.0 that only allowed users to read. I have also used computers where a floppy disk holds a few mb files. In web 1.0, you could see only static websites and users couldn't interact with these websites. These websites were only for reading and your suggestions couldn't be added anywhere. Just use and go off technology. Now today from 2000, we have web 2.0, where we can read and write too. It's the current version where people can interact with images, videos, and systems. You have the freedom to add your suggestions and thoughts on the web. Web 2.0 is also known as the social web because it's the first-time people have interacted with each other at a global scale. You can also say it global village. But it's clear that people could add suggestions and feedback accordingly with the platform guidelines. Like on Facebook or Instagram, hate and offensive words are really prohibited to maintain a balance of harmony, love and respect. Basically, web 2.0 is centralized with social methods. If there are conflicts between users and platforms, the platform decision will be final. The users will have to accept this to facilitate interaction. Now we have web 3.0, the internet of the future.

Web 3.0 is the third generation of the internet that focuses on decentralisation. As we all know Facebook, WhatsApp, Google and other companies use our data to facilitate our interactions and choices but in web 3.0, there's no mediator or any centralized platforms that can misuse our data. It's a platform of great transparency and control. It will aid us to prevent piracy and protect our data from getting misused. All we can say is, it's an intelligent system. We all know, most of the books get published on centralised platforms and sometimes books get pirated. Web 3.0 protects our data to give only to people we want and rest, no one will get any information about it. Sometimes video courses and movies also get leaked online, and people and companies suffer. Damn, it's the internet of the future because data leaks are still the hot potato on the internet. Web 3.0 will also support the Cryptocurrency systems because to buy and sell, we would need Crypto.

We call web 3.0 intelligent because it's an automatic processed information. Like if we input information, the machine will read and analyse the information automatically, so there's less chance to get the data misused. It's the second life where we would get connected 24 hours with high transparency and control. With web 3.0, people are also talking about web 4.0, where our own clone can be created and it's popularly known as the digital alter ego. Intelligent machines will have good control of information and connect real and virtual worlds in real time. Additionally, we have web 5.0 as well, in which we will develop computers that will interact with human beings. Web 5.0 will be based on sensory and emotive webs where computers will understand humans logically and emotionally. We know, it will be the complex level of the web.

FINAL VERDICT ON BLOCKCHAIN TECHNOLOGY

In our opinion, a modern technology should not discard the conventional technology because by discarding the old, we discard their advantages as well. Like with the introduction of mobiles, we can't discard calculators, so that we can have the advantage of using them without electricity. There's no denying, blockchain technology is the future to adopt decentralization and freedom but with the versatility of public and security of our nation, centralisation is also significant to maintain the country's position financially and mentally. There was never a 100% positive stake for anything and our world works with majority and majority can be right or wrong. Till now, there has been dissimilarities of views among various nations. Because of Cryptocurrency, blockchain technology was introduced and now because of Cryptocurrency, people are discarding the blockchain technology. It's miserable. *The first impression of Blockchain is conflicting, and we need more discussions to understand why we should leave everything decentralized and how the world will grow with that. We also need to leave authority to the government to take decisions at the national level. Decentralisation is a responsibility, and without responsibility and confidence, the world can't work.* Someone has to be responsible, and to get the proper implementation of Blockchain, people should feel the responsibilities so that just because of a few, the whole world would not have to suffer.

In the whole world, the government is understanding Blockchain, but absorbing its classification will take some time. *Blockchain is undeniably the future of the human world and web 5.0 will be the smartest move of any century. Remember that!*

About the Author

DEEPAK GUPTA is pre-eminently known for writing plain sailing, meticulous, and pragmatic Self-Help books. He's the author of **more than forty books** including **10 Principles to Beat Failure** that won **Google Best Choice 2018** & became **Top Seller on Google Play Store in 2019**. He has been garnering much acclaim for his **30 Minutes Read & 10 Principles Series**. Till now, he has received **500k+ readership** & **a lot of appreciation** from all over the world. He believes in writing & living best exceptional content from his subconscious mind. He loves to observe, absorb, and write on various social issues, inspirational truthful words, short stories, and heart whelming poetry. Also, he has travelled to many places in India like Manali, Rajasthan, Goa, Kolkata, Madhya Pradesh, Jammu, Dalhousie, and Mussoorie to bring originality in his work. He *releases new short books every month* to get readers to connect with the truth of life.

Deepak Gupta received his post-graduation degree from **Delhi School of Economics**. Also, when he's not writing, he can be found wandering on his **exquisite terrace garden**. He lives with his family in **Delhi, India**.

Keep in touch with Deepak via the web:
Instagram @authordeepakgupta
Facebook: facebook.com/authordeepakgupta
Twitter @authordeepakgup

Don't miss out!

Visit the website below and you can sign up to receive emails whenever Deepak Gupta publishes a new book. There's no charge and no obligation.

https://books2read.com/r/B-A-AQXE-TCAWB

BOOKS2READ

Connecting independent readers to independent writers.

Did you love *Blockchain Technology: The Future*? Then you should read *10 Principles To Beat Failure: Illustrated Enhanced Edition*[1] by Deepak Gupta!

DEEPAK GUPTA[2]

Implement drop in the ocean of knowledge and you can make ocean out of the drop.

Life is not as plain-sailing as we think. It has the habit to create hurdles in our path. Whenever we try to do something great, people will come and laugh at us. This is the universal law. 10 Principles to Beat Failure can help you with the following Concepts & Problems:

How to be Happy Consistently.Problems related Truths &

1. https://books2read.com/u/m0gvyY

2. https://books2read.com/u/m0gvyY

Myths.How to execute plans.How to feel satisfied at the end of day.How to set your Goals Strongly.How to say NO to unwanted tasks.How to understand Rights & Wrongs to Success.Why we fail at execution of Goals.Do's & Don'ts in Morning Schedule.How to understand your Satisfaction Level.How to be Successful Consistently.How to build Bullet-Proof Success.How to Celebrate Success.How to Increase Knowledge.The Attributes of Visionary People.How to Free your Mind.The Classical Conditioning of Life.How to Work in Panic.How to Link Appreciation with Results.How to attract more people to our products.How to not be a Rat.The Bandersnatch to take Best Life Decisions.How to get more ideas everyday.The Game of Mindset.How to decide our Mind Feed.

What to expect in NEW ILLUSTRATED ENHANCED EDITION 2021:

★ **Added 32 New Chapters, Bonuses, and Illustrations which will help readers to understand Success and Failure Principles in much Simplified Manner.**

★ **Revised All Principles with Best Possible Practical Practices.**

Every day is the day to get up again and to learn something innovative and creative. To become a superior person, we should learn to observe our nature and understand the latent power inside it. Our power lies in to understand the invincible love and greatest power of our mind. But how much we focus to create our mind happy and healthy? Have we ever thought of this matter? How many negative thoughts have unconsciously latent in our mind? How we waste our energy every day because of our purposeless negative thoughts. We never focus on the depth of our mind as we always busy in our run and races &

money and faces. Being good is not only a matter of the good heart but also the matter of the beautiful mind to cope up with the end number of life failures. If you want to become cheery and to take the right decision, then you should understand the beautiful nerves of your mind.

10 Principles To Beat Failure includes ten mind boggling principles that will change your life forever and boost you to achieve your dreams and aspirations at any stage of life.

We have to ask questions, not because we want to know the answers. Answers don't exist universally. They exist in the form to make fit in our life. What make us satisfied is our answers.

Read more at https://www.authordeepakgupta.com.

Also by Deepak Gupta

15 Minutes Read
Common Sense in the 21st Century

30 Minutes Read
How To Deal With Haters
One Second Rule: How to take Right Decisions quickly
without Thinking too Much
Hard Decisions Easy Life: Bandersnatch & The World of
Possibilities
Sell Your Talent: How to Convert Talent into Money along
with the Personality Development
Ideas & Origami
The Anti-Suicidal Self Help Book
The Therapy of Peace: Illustrated Edition
The Rules of Being Highly Productive
How to Think Everyday
Bedtime Thinker
The Rules of Being Highly Skillful
Blockchain Technology: The Future

Power
The Power of Universe
The Power of Nothing: They say and We do

Year of Short Stories
But She Didn't Come

Standalone
Inspiring Life
Zero Degree: An Icy Thriller
She: She Heals Everything
10 Principles To Beat Failure: Illustrated Enhanced Edition
Beta 2020
10 Principles To Love Yourself
How To Heal Yourself
She: She heals everything
Skyfall: Your Heart Will Fall Too
The Girl With No Dreams
The Pigeon With Broken Legs: Modern Classics Children
Story
Average Mind: The World is not the Wonder. It's the Wonder
which makes your World
Being Busy Is Not Always Productive: Stop Wasting your Time
at the Wrong Place

Happiness Without Cause: Why Happiness was easy in the 19th Century but not in the 21st Century

Alone Than Lonely: How to Live Life without Attachment & Enjoy your Company

The Lost Child

The Power Pack of Short Stories: Box Set of Crime, Thriller & Suspense Stories

Earth 2200

Amazon Kindle & Google Play ebooks Pricing System: Maximize Your ebooks Sales

5 Principles To Dig Out Success

????: Udhaar

The Little Book of Wise Quotes

Deepak Gupta Collection: The Complete Self Help Book (2015-2020)

Revenge

Revolutionary Love: Friendship-Love-Revenge: A Novel

The Man Who Forgets

Watch for more at https://www.authordeepakgupta.com.